Houses and homes

Contents

Teachers' notes	1	Different homes	19
Parts of a house	5	Christmas parcels – 1	20
The front door	6	Christmas parcels – 2	21
Animal homes	7	Different rooms – 1	22
The letter	8	Different rooms – 2	23
Lucy's day	9	Pets	24
Pet jigsaws	10	On the fence	25
Machine jigsaws	11	Catching the burglar	26
In the garden	12	Cat on the roof	27
Family breakfast	13	House and garden – 1	28
Ben's house	14	House and garden – 2	29
Where we live	15	Family size – 1	30
Riddles – 1	16	Family size – 2	31
Riddles – 2	17	The storm	32
In the home	18		

Teachers' notes

The activities in this book aim to support the implementation of the National Curriculum for geography at Levels 1 to 3. These activities are not designed as teaching tools in their own right, but rather they offer the opportunity to practise newly-acquired knowledge and skills. It is important to explain the purpose of each activity at the start so that children can focus on that aspect of the task.

Aims of this book

● To highlight the many different types of houses and homes.
● To develop children's knowledge and vocabulary in relation to houses and homes.
● To introduce children to key ideas and knowledge about houses and homes.
● To provide opportunities to practise basic skills in English and mathematics within the context of a study of houses and homes.
● To encourage children to think about the address of their home and why it is important that each home has one.
● To look at the types of activities which take place at home.

Reproducing the activities

Most activities can be photocopied on to white paper, but in some cases (such as 8, 10, 11, 20 and 21) copying on to coloured paper may well be beneficial. Similarly copying on to card for pages 10, 11, 20 and 21 can provide a valuable resource, especially if the sheets are covered in clear, sticky plastic.

Geographical background

The study of houses and homes is a fundamental part of the local geography of every child. Houses and homes are the basis from which the children venture out to explore the environment. In the early years, places such as school, the park or the shops are located in relation to the home, that is how far or near they are, in terms of both time and distance. The home helps children to make sense of the rest of their environment and gives them a sense of perspective.

Activities which focus on homes, particularly the children's own homes will need sensitive handling. It is important to stress that not all children have two parents and live in a four-bedroom detached house! Each type of home (caravan, flat, maisonette, terraced house, semi-detached, etc) has its own merits and the activities in this book are designed to preclude any value judgements on the relative merits of the different types. Rather, the emphasis is on everyday activities or information which will be common to all homes, irrespective of the type of building.

The activities also include ideas about animal homes and this extends to pets (pages 7, 10 and 19). The aim is to encourage children to think about other creatures' need for homes, as well as dealing with the sharing of our homes with our pets. Similarly, key ideas on how activities in the home change throughout the day (page 9) are an important part of developing children's knowledge about houses and homes.

● ESSENTIALS FOR GEOGRAPHY: Houses and homes

Other important points are developing ideas about the different rooms in homes, their different purposes and how this requires different furniture (pages 22 and 23).

At this stage it is important for children to develop knowledge and ideas about their own homes and those of their classmates. Studies of homes in other countries (see *Hot Places* in this series) and other environments should come later once the groundwork has been established.

Notes on individual activities

Page 5: Parts of a house

Aim: to familiarise the children with the names of key parts of the house.
Preparation and practice: before they start the activity, encourage the children to describe the picture and to name the different parts of the house.
Extension: draw a picture of another type of home, such as a flat and name its different parts.

Page 6: The front door

Aim: to encourage children to look more carefully and critically at aspects of their home, starting with the front door.
Preparation and practice: be sure children can identify the main features of the door shown, including the letter box, number and door knob. Talk to them about the front door of their own home and what features they will need to include on their picture.
Extension: ask the children to name their favourite/least favourite feature of their front door. Draw the front door of a friend.

Page 7: Animal homes

Aim: to encourage children to think about the different types of homes that animals use.
Preparation and practice: discuss class pets such as gerbils or goldfish and the homes in which they live, as well as the animals and homes shown in the pictures and animals in the wild.
Extension: on the pictures of animal homes mark features which keep out the rain and keep in the heat.

Page 8: The letter

Aim: to ensure that children know their own address and understand what the parts of the address mean.
Preparation and practice: show the children a large version of a letter addressed to the school, highlighting the different parts of the address – name, number, street, town and county. Discuss the reason for including all this information in an address, then look at their own addresses. In some cases it may be best to work backwards from the county to the street.
Extension: address letters to friends or relatives.

Page 9: Lucy's day

Aim: to highlight regular movements to and from the home and how these vary with time.
Preparation and practice: discuss with the children what they do at different times of the day – from getting up in the morning to going to bed at night. They can sequence the pictures in a straight line, or in a circle like a clock face, linked to specific times.
Extension: draw a picture to show a school day and a day at the weekend. How are they different?

Pages 10 and 11: Pet jigsaws/ Machine jigsaws

Aim: to encourage children to think about the contents of homes – the things that are found inside besides themselves and their parents.
Preparation and practice: the pictures at the top of the page should help children to match the jigsaw pieces.
Extension: make jigsaws of furniture at home for friends to complete.

Pages 12 and 13: In the garden/ Family breakfast

Aim: to highlight the range of activities that take place in homes, and encourage children to imagine events and conversations which might take place.
Preparation and practice: discuss what is happening in each scene and what the people might be saying before starting the activity.
Extension: suggest what else the people might be saying. Draw other scenes in the home, such as people watching TV or playing computer games, and write speech bubbles to show what they are saying.

Page 14: Ben's house

Aim: to link the three-dimensional and two-dimensional images of house shapes and enable children to see these links more clearly.
Preparation and practice: colour in the roof, front door and windows then cut out the shape and make the house.
Extension: use the houses to make a street, or village, on a layout which shows features such as a stream, or a hill. Can the children draw other shapes to cut out and assemble?

Page 15: Where we live

Aim: to encourage children to consider the wide range of different types of houses and homes.

Preparation and practice: discuss what the pictures show (i.e. different types of house) and point out the main differences, such as flats being in a block, and semi-detached being joined together. This is necessary to ensure that children can correctly identify their own home.
Extension: ask the children to draw the houses that are in their street. Do they know someone who lives in the type of house that has not been matched?

Pages 16 and 17: Riddles – 1 and 2

Aim: to encourage children to consider the different types of equipment found in the home and their various uses.
Preparation and practice: discuss the characteristics of various household objects and go on to write short descriptive texts based on everyday items found in the home.
Extension: write riddles for friends using objects found in the home.

Pages 18 and 19: In the home/ Different homes

Aim: to highlight the different functions and equipment of different parts of the home.
Preparation and practice: discuss what is shown in each picture before starting these activities. Explain to the children that they need to cut out the sentences and stick them under the appropriate picture.
Extension: draw other pictures of rooms and of homes and write sentences to go with them.

Pages 20 and 21: Christmas parcels – 1 and 2

Aim: to enable children to think about sorting parcels in the context of a small group.
Preparation and practice: it may be helpful to let the children practise sorting using dummy parcels labelled with the names of children in the class. Once they understand what is involved they can cut out the parcels and deliver them to the correct person.
Extension: write letters to the people in the picture and sort the letters.

Pages 22 and 23: Different rooms – 1 and 2

Aim: to highlight the different types of furniture to be found in different rooms.
Preparation and practice: the objects from Different rooms – 1 need to be cut out and matched with the diagram on Different rooms – 2. The teacher may want to point out that some objects, like the portable radio, could be found in both rooms, and discuss with children those objects that are specific to particular rooms.
Extension: draw pictures of other objects found in the home and stick them on to the diagram.

Page 24: Pets

Aim: to develop children's sorting abilities.
Preparation and practice: encourage the children to choose their own categories when sorting out the pets, for example two legs or four legs, stripes, dots, and so on.
Extension: draw other animals which are found at home, for example gerbils, budgies, goldfish, and sort them.

Page 25: On the fence

Aim: to encourage children to look at the many different types of boundaries to be found around homes and properties.
Preparation and practice: talk to the children about the type of fences found around their home. In particular, discuss what such fences are made of, such as hedges, wood, bricks or concrete.
Extension: discuss why fences are useful and why they can also be a nuisance.

Page 26: Catching the burglar

Aim: to look at dramatic activities which may take place around the home.
Preparation and practice: before the children start to write the story discuss with them what is happening in each picture. Give some thought to a title for the story and how this might affect the ending.
Extension: invent other dramatic activities that may take place around the home.

Page 27: Cat on the roof

Aim: to develop awareness of some of the dangers around the home.
Preparation and practice: point out to the children the need to relate the pictures they draw to the text. Similarly, stress the importance of writing concisely what the printed picture shows in clear, short sentences. Discuss how the story might develop and which details can be represented in the drawings and which by text.
Extension: write sentences and draw pictures of other events around the home, for example the chip pan catches fire!

Pages 28 and 29: House and garden – 1 and 2

Aim: to develop awareness of scale in relation to sorting elements inside the home and in the garden.
Preparation and practice: discuss what is shown in each picture and how they will need to be arranged to fit on the Carroll diagram.
Extension: draw other different-sized objects from house and garden and stick them on the Carroll diagram.

Pages 30 and 31: Family size – 1 and 2

Aim: to highlight the way in which the scale of items in the home is related to the people who live there.

Preparation and practice: point out that babies do not eat with a knife and fork, but use a small spoon, how they sit in a high chair and sleep in a cot. Discuss similarities and differences between adults and children of four or five in terms of furniture and cutlery. On the Carroll diagram one item fits into each space.

Extension: draw other items for the people on the chart and stick them on the Carroll diagram.

Page 32: The storm

Aim: to encourage children to think about how houses protect them from the weather, and how extremes of weather can damage the houses.

Preparation and practice: discuss with the children the ways in which houses provide protection from the weather – the walls, roof, windows and door. Look at the effects of very severe weather and how families might cope with the resulting problems.

Extension: draw the effects of a flood on a house built on a river bank.

National Curriculum: Geography

The activities in this book support the following requirements of the PoS for KS1 from the geography National Curriculum:

Geographical Skills
Pupils should be taught to develop and use the following geographical skills:
- following directions, including the terms up, down, near, far, left, right;
- using and making different kinds of maps and plans, both real and imaginary, at a variety of scales, using pictures/ symbols and other aspects of a key;
- following a route on a plan or a map.

Places and Themes
Pupils should be taught:
- about the main physical and/or human features of the localities;
- about how land and buildings are used;
- about changes in the environment of the locality;
- about ways in which the quality of that environment can be sustained and improved.

Scottish 5 - 14 Curriculum: Environmental studies – Social subjects

Attainment outcome	Strand	Target	Level
Understanding people and places	Knowledge and understanding	Aspects of the physical and built environment; locations, linkages and networks; using maps.	A
	Interpreting and evaluation	From recorded information answer simple questions about context and meaning.	A
Healthy and safe living	Knowledge and understanding	Safety in the environment.	A
	Taking action on health and safety	Investigate which people are important to health and safety.	A

See inside back cover for Northern Ireland Curriculum links

● ESSENTIALS FOR GEOGRAPHY: Houses and homes

● Name _____

Parts of a house

● Can you match the words with the objects in the picture?

chimney   **roof**   **door**

wall   **window**   **drainpipe**

● Colour in the house.

ESSENTIALS FOR GEOGRAPHY: Houses and Homes

● Name _____

The front door

- This is Mary's front door.

- Colour the letter box red.

- Colour the door knob black.

- Colour each of the panels.

- Now draw your own front door in the space below.

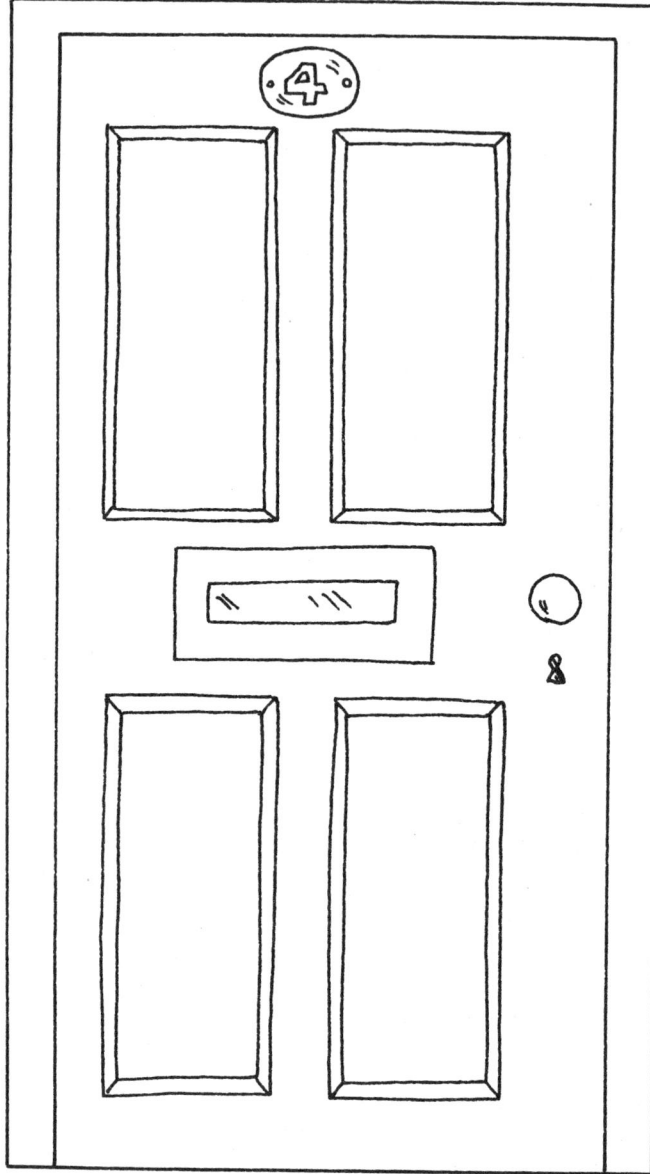

● ESSENTIALS FOR GEOGRAPHY: Houses and Homes

6

● **Name** _____

Animal homes

● Draw a line linking each animal or bird with its home.

● Now draw another animal in the box on the left and draw its home next to it. Can you think of others to draw?

● ESSENTIALS FOR GEOGRAPHY: Houses and Homes

● Name _____

The letter

● Fill in the address on the letter.

● In box A write your name.

● In boxes B and C write the number of your house and the name of the road.

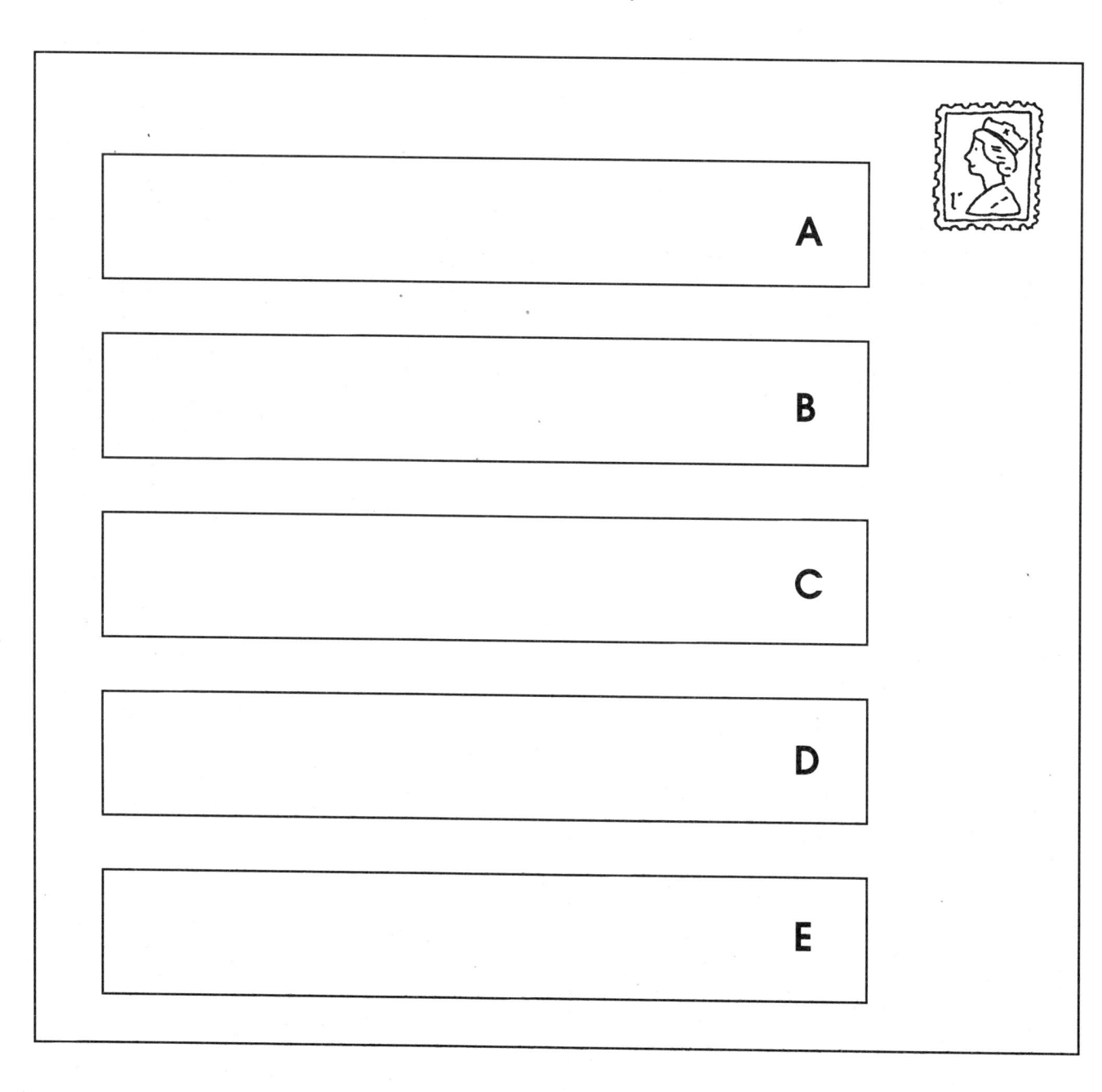

● In box D write the name of the town.

● In box E write the name of the county.

A

B

C

D

E

● ESSENTIALS FOR GEOGRAPHY: Houses and Homes

Name _____

Lucy's day

The pictures show how Lucy spends her day.

● Colour them in then cut them out and put them in order.

ESSENTIALS FOR GEOGRAPHY: Houses and Homes

Name _____

Pet jigsaws

● Two pet jigsaws have been muddled together. Cut out the pieces and complete the jigsaws.

ESSENTIALS FOR GEOGRAPHY: Houses and Homes

● Name _____

Machine jigsaws

● Two machine jigsaws have been muddled together. Cut out the pieces and complete the jigsaws.

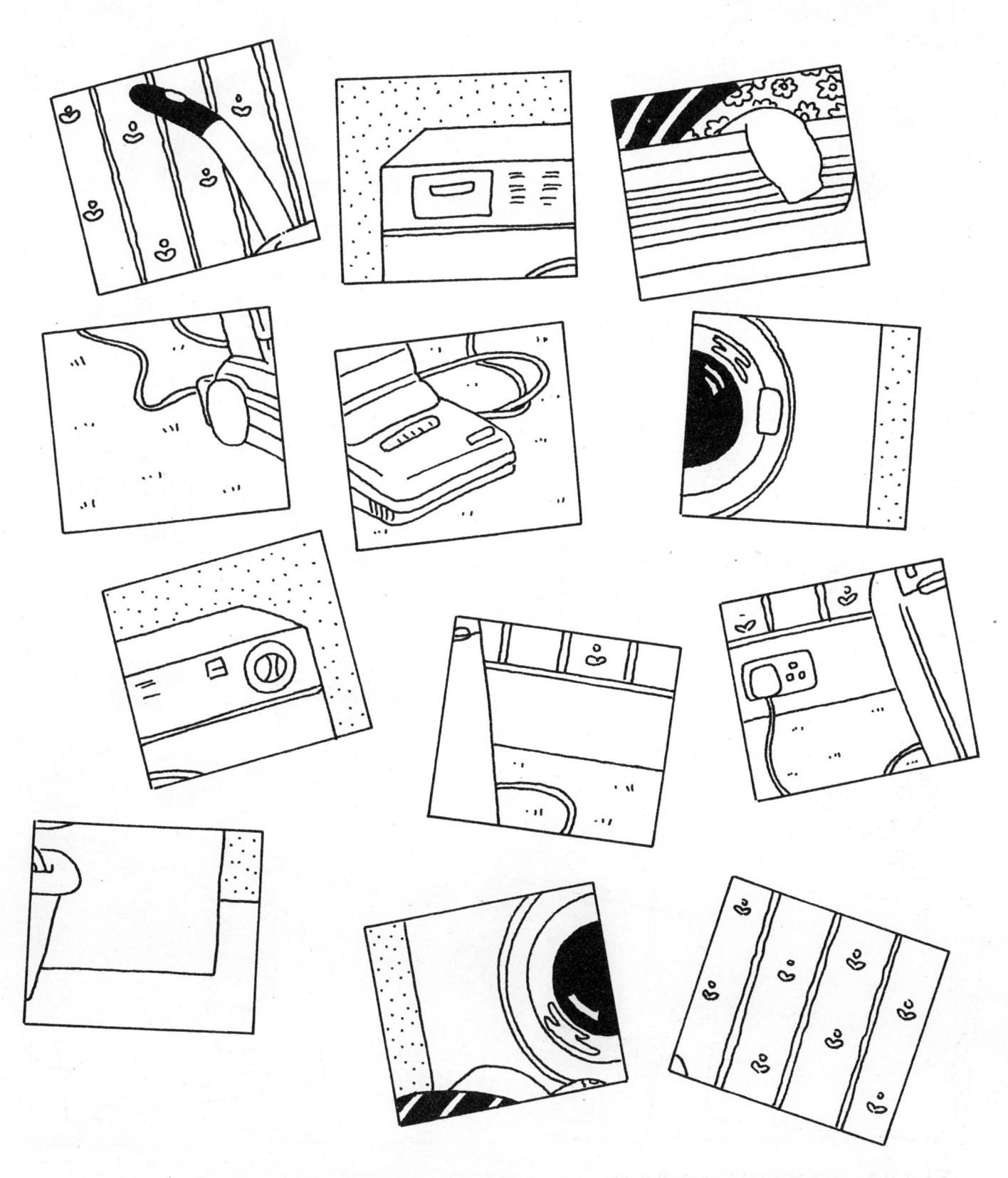

ESSENTIALS FOR GEOGRAPHY: Houses and Homes

11

● Name _____

In the garden

● Look at the picture. What are the people saying?
Write their words in the speech bubbles.

ESSENTIALS FOR GEOGRAPHY: Houses and Homes   12

Name _____

Family breakfast

● Look at the picture. What are the people saying? Write their words in the speech bubbles.

ESSENTIALS FOR GEOGRAPHY: Houses and Homes   13

● Name _____

Ben's house

● Colour in the house below.

● Now cut it out and cut slits to make tabs.

● Fold along the dotted lines.

● Now can you make the house as shown in the picture on the right?

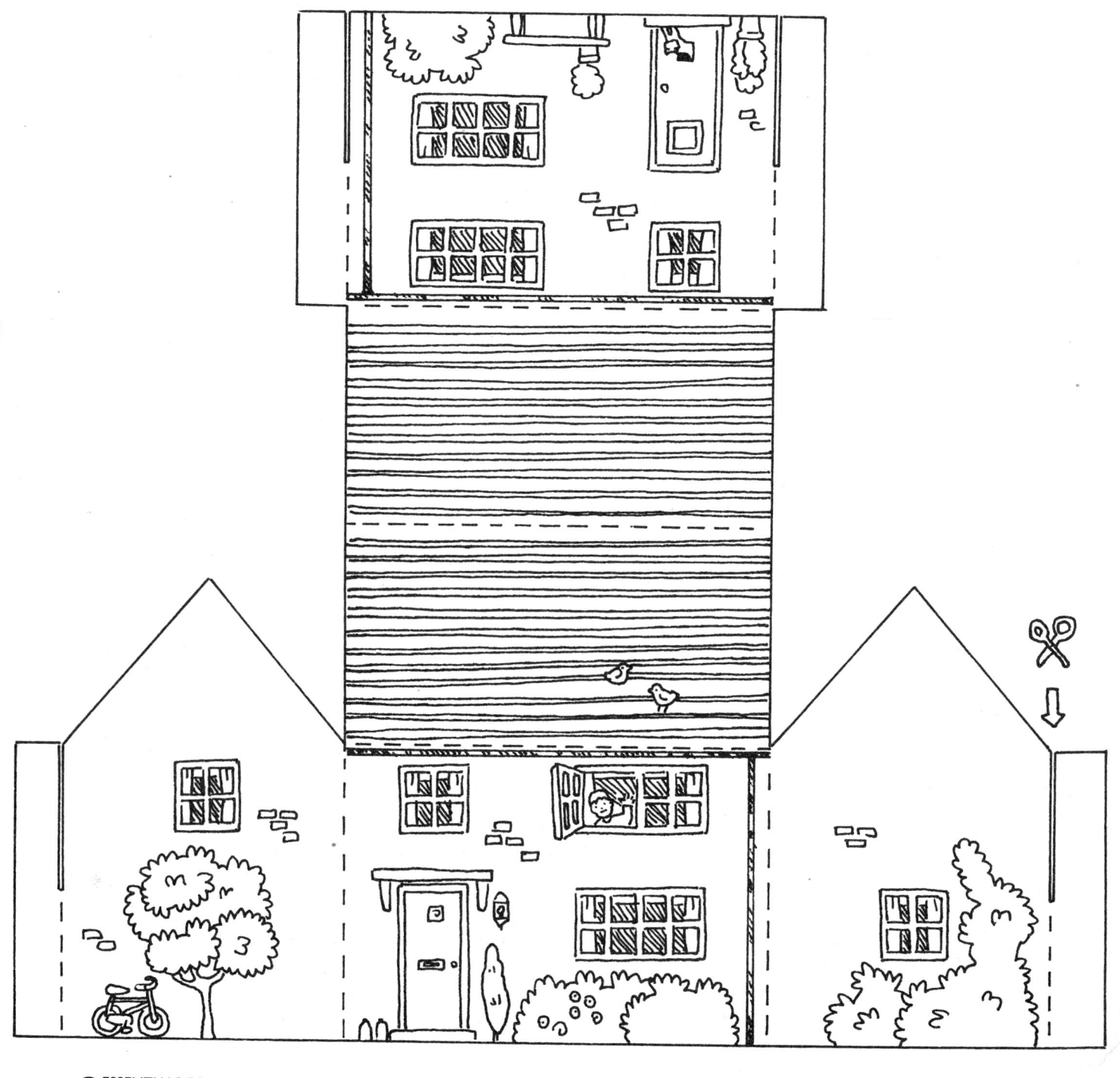

ESSENTIALS FOR GEOGRAPHY: Houses and Homes   14

● Name _____

Where we live

- Draw a picture of yourself in the first box.

- Now draw a friend in each of the other boxes.

- Match the people with the type of home in which they live.

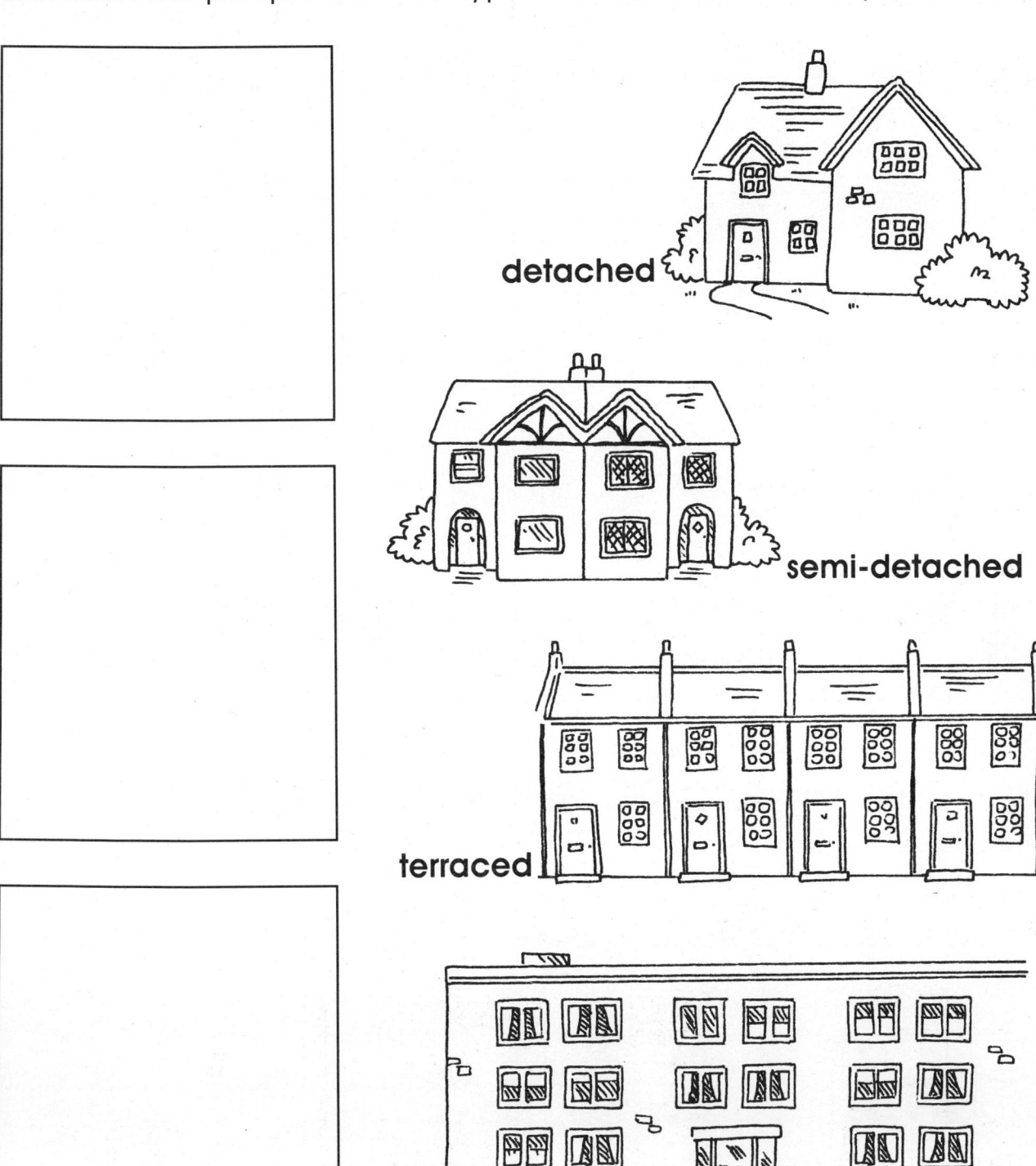

detached

semi-detached

terraced

flats

ESSENTIALS FOR GEOGRAPHY: Houses and Homes   15

● Name _____

Riddles – 1

● Read the riddles and write in the answers.

I suck up dirt.	I have four wheels.
I use electricity.	You can drive me.
You can push me.	People go to school in me.
I am a _____	I am a _____

● Can you write in the riddles for the objects below?

_____

_____

_____

I am a washing machine

_____

_____

_____

I am a telephone

_____

_____

_____

I am a television

_____

_____

_____

I am a bed

● ESSENTIALS FOR GEOGRAPHY: Houses and Homes

● Name _____

Riddles – 2

● Read the riddles and write in the answers.

I boil water.	I keep people warm.
I switch myself off.	They wear me on their head.
I plug into the electricity.	I am made of cloth.
I am a _____	I am a _____

● Can you write in the riddles for the objects below?

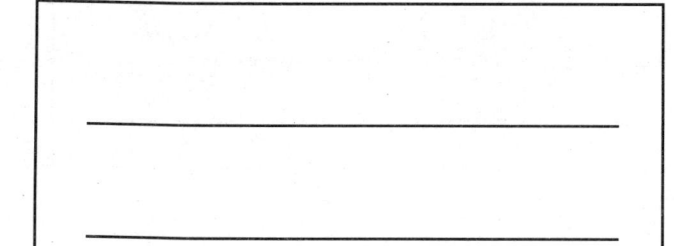

I am a toaster

I am a radio

I am a computer

I am an iron

ESSENTIALS FOR GEOGRAPHY: Houses and Homes

● Name _____

In the home

● Look at the pictures and sentences below.

● Now cut out the sentences and match them to the pictures.

```
I am in the bedroom.
I am wearing pyjamas.
```

```
I am in the kitchen.
I am thirsty so I am having
a drink.
```

```
I am in the garage.
The car is not going well
so I am repairing it.
```

```
I am in the study. I am
working on my computer.
```

● ESSENTIALS FOR GEOGRAPHY: Houses and Homes

● Name _____

Different homes

● Look at the pictures and sentences below.

● Now cut out the sentences and match them to the pictures.

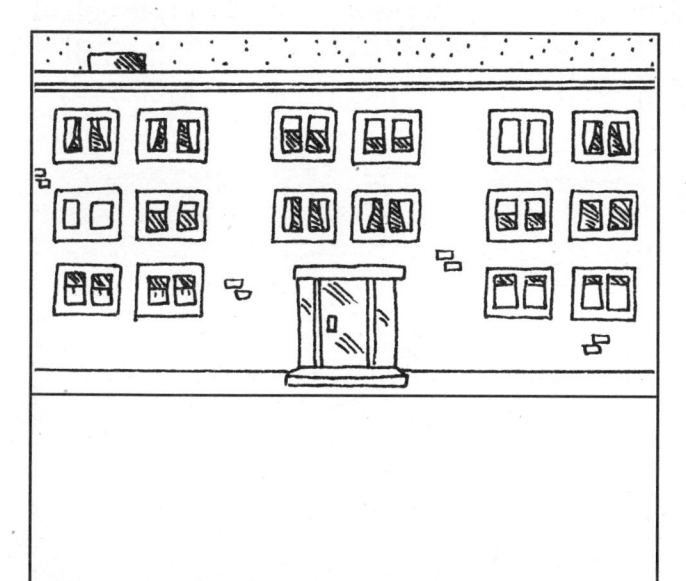

I live in a cottage.
It has a thatched roof.

I live in a flat.
It is on the third floor
of our block.

I live in a terraced house.
It is joined to lots of
other houses.

I live in a cage.
It has bars and a wheel.

ESSENTIALS FOR GEOGRAPHY: Houses and Homes

Name _____

Christmas parcels – 1

• Use this sheet with Christmas parcels – 2.

• These are Christmas presents for Class One.
Cut them out and sort the parcels.

PAUL ALI PAUL
ALI PAUL
PAUL PAUL ALI
MARY ALI
PAUL MARY PAUL

ESSENTIALS FOR GEOGRAPHY: Houses and Homes   20

● Name _____

Christmas parcels – 2

Use this sheet with Christmas parcels – 1.

● Help the children collect their parcels. Stick them in the correct sacks.

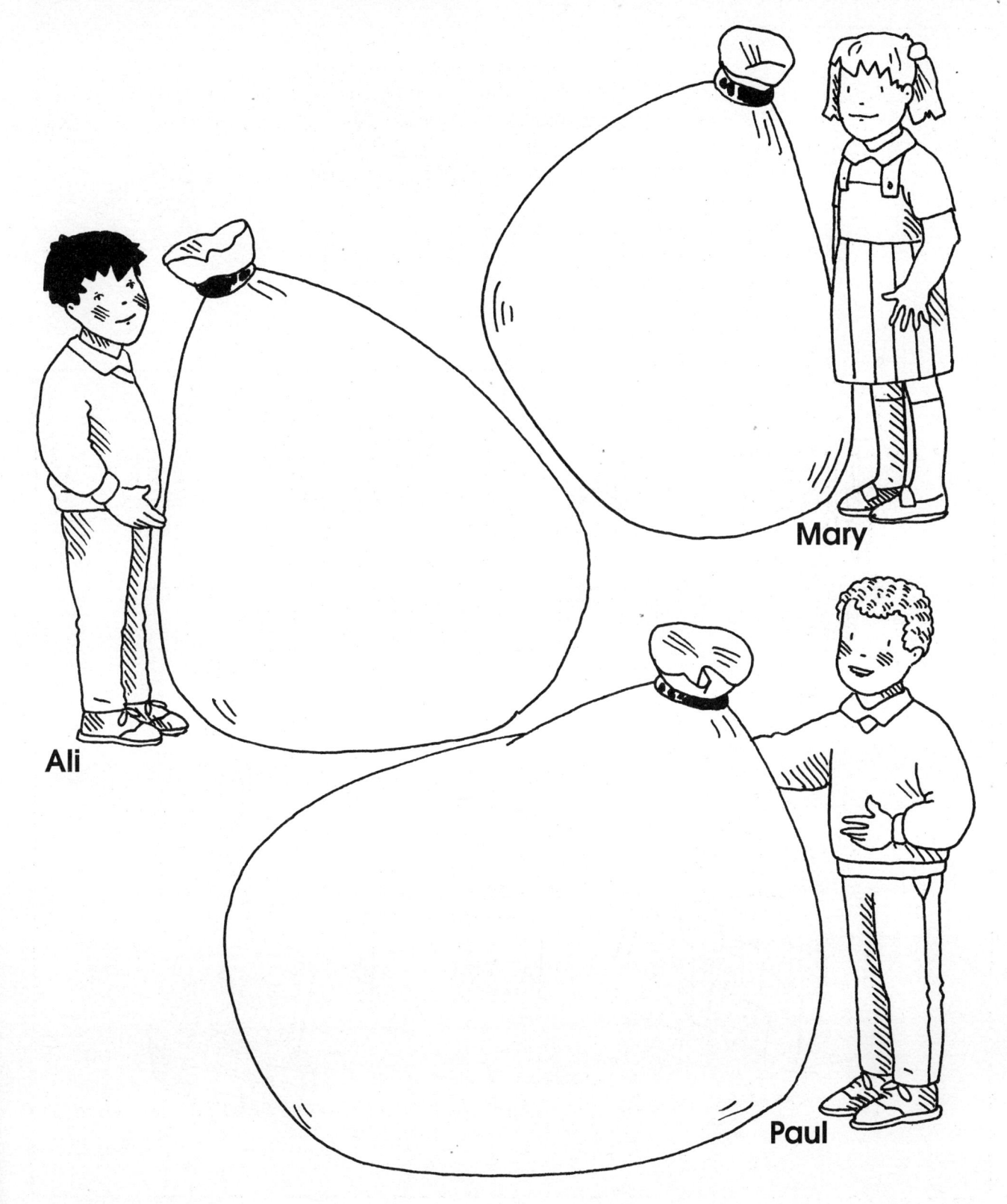

Ali

Mary

Paul

● ESSENTIALS FOR GEOGRAPHY: Houses and Homes

● Name _____

Different rooms – 1

● Colour in the objects below.

● Now cut them out and stick them into the room where they belong on Different rooms – 2.

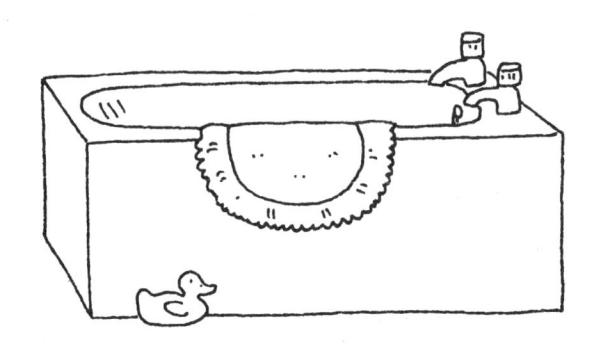

ESSENTIALS FOR GEOGRAPHY: Houses and Homes

22

● Name _____

Different rooms – 2

● Use this sheet with Different rooms – 1.

I am in the bathroom. Stick in all the objects you find here.

I am in the living room. Stick in all the objects you find here.

ESSENTIALS FOR GEOGRAPHY: Houses and Homes

● Name _____

Pets

● Cut out the pets and sort them into groups.

● ESSENTIALS FOR GEOGRAPHY: Houses and Homes

● Name _____

On the fence

● Look at the pictures and words below.
Can you match the words with the correct picture?

tall wooden fence   brick wall   chain link fence

hedge   railings   low wooden fence

● Colour in each type of fence.

● Now draw some other types of fence.

ESSENTIALS FOR GEOGRAPHY: Houses and Homes   25

Catching the burglar

- Look at the pictures below. Draw a picture in the empty box to complete the story.

- Now write the story shown in the pictures and give it a title.

ESSENTIALS FOR GEOGRAPHY: Houses and Homes

Name _____

Cat on the roof

● Draw in the missing pictures and write the missing text. Now finish the story off in the last box.

One day the cat climbed the tree. Then she jumped on to the roof of the house.

Suddenly the ladder fell away and dad was stuck on the roof. Then the fire engine arrived.

● ESSENTIALS FOR GEOGRAPHY: Houses and Homes   27

● Name _____

House and garden – 1

● Colour in the objects below.

● Match the labels with the objects. Now look at the Carroll diagram on House and garden – 2.

wardrobe	settee	trowel
tree	telephone	radio	bucket
lawn mower	cup and saucer

● ESSENTIALS FOR GEOGRAPHY: Houses and Homes

● Name _____

House and garden – 2

Use this sheet with House and garden – 1.

● Sort the objects into the correct groups and write their names in the diagram below.

	in the house	in the garden
large		
small		

ESSENTIALS FOR GEOGRAPHY: Houses and Homes

Name _____

Family size – 1

● Look at the pictures below.

● Can you match the labels with the objects?
Now look at the Carroll diagram on Family size – 2.

baby's spoon	cot	small chair
large chair	large bed	baby's high chair
small bed	small knife and fork	large knife and fork

ESSENTIALS FOR GEOGRAPHY: Houses and Homes   30

Family size – 2

Use this sheet with Family size – 1.

● Sort the objects into the correct groups and write their names in the diagram below.

	bed	things to eat with	chair
mum			
child aged 4-5			
baby			

ESSENTIALS FOR GEOGRAPHY: Houses and Homes

Name _____

The storm

● Look at the pictures below. Draw a picture in the empty box to complete the story.

● Write out the story shown in the pictures and give your story a title.

ESSENTIALS FOR GEOGRAPHY: Houses and Homes